I Am Your Connection

I Am Your Connection:

Love Poems for Your Beloved

Anne Pepper

Chrysalid Books
Vancouver, Canada

Text copyright © 2023 Anne Pepper
Illustrations copyright ©2023 Simona Sasarman

All rights reserved.

No part of this book may be reproduced in any form or by any electronic or mechanical means, including information storage and retrieval systems, without the prior written permission of the author, except in the case of brief quotations used in articles and reviews.

To request permissions, contact chrysalidbooks@gmail.com.

ISBN 978-1-7388331-0-8

Published by Chrysalid Books, Vancouver, Canada.
Typeset in PF Beau Sans Pro and Learning Curve.
First paperback edition January 2024.
Available in eBook edition.

Front cover design by Kate Flett.
Inside illustrations by Simona Sasarman, sasarmanst@yahoo.ca.
Interior design and layout by Becky Fulker, Kubera Book Design.

I Am Your Connection: Love Poems for Your Beloved
by Anne Pepper. Vancouver, BC, 2024.

AnnePepper.com

Dedicated to F.T.
Long may you reign.

Just as the sun shines adoration onto the earth, and the earth receives it and replies with abundance, there is a natural harmony in our most intimate and committed relationship that mirrors the harmony in nature. May this harmony flow through us as we see the Divine in our partner and our beloved relationship as a microcosm of our own relationship with the Divine.

Contents

A Palace of Glass	3
The Visitor	5
I See in You a Wildness	7
There is No Salt	9
The Nature of Love	11
Chameleon	13
I Am Your Connection	15
The Genie in a Bottle	17
The Body is a Temple	19
We Are Walking in a Cathedral	21
The Crystal	23
The Principle	25
Immortal	27
The Silent Verse	29
900 years	31
A Rose and its Thorns	33
Bring me Beauty	35
There is a Portal	37
Where We are Going	39
The Sky and the Earth	41
The Summoning	43
Hands	45
Sandcastles	47
The Totem	49
Somehow You Discovered this Trick	51

Did I ever tell you	53
Everything That Comes to Me	55
The Earth on My Skin	57
The Other Way Around	59
Guru and Teacher	61
Still Being Consumed	63
The Clouds Here	65
I Have No Advice	67
In the Garden	69
The Clouds	71
Two Halves and a Whole	73
Where is Your Vulnerability	75
The Flames and the Fire	77
You're Going to Cleanse the Last Part of Me	79
We Shouldn't Talk Too Much	81
Nothing can keep us apart	83
Returning to Our Homes	85
The Tap Drips	87
I Write You a Love Poem	89
I See How in All Things	91
The Flower and the Woman	93
Watching	95
Paradise Lost	97
From the Author	98
About the Author	99

Poems

A Palace of Glass

Being with you
Is like coming home
But not to the house of my childhood
Instead
I have crossed the threshold
into a palace of glass
Where everywhere I turn
I see myself
Where I can access
    All of me
    All at once
(If you've never been here, I highly recommend it).
It's as though
I have no borders
That I belong to Life
More than to myself
And in this place I become
A diamond
With a thousand aspects
Each side carved
To reflect more light.
And so, after my distant travels
I am home at last
With you by my side
I can now begin to reflect the light
Outwards.

The Visitor

Can you feel
Under this cloudless sky
That it is never
Just you and me
That we are never alone.
Even here
In this empty room
It is not just me and you.
We have become aware
Of how tenderly
We must treat each other
So as not to harm the visitor.
So from now on
Let's set the table for three
Why pretend
It is any other way?

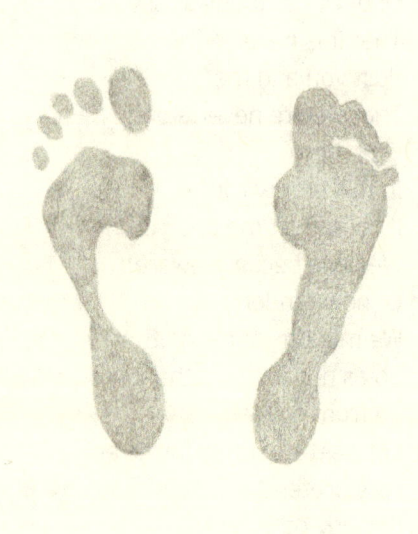

I See in You a Wildness

I see in you a wildness
That culture cannot tame
A panther in a cage
With the door left open
You exist in this world
Yet flourish in the other
Your instinct propels you forward
Prowling when the path is clear
It is your stealth at the unseen
That draws me to you
Your wildness and your mystery
Woven into life
So that we stand here
Talking of other things
While onwards you prowl
Lighting the flame in me
So that now I clearly see
I need the panther in you
To join the one in me.

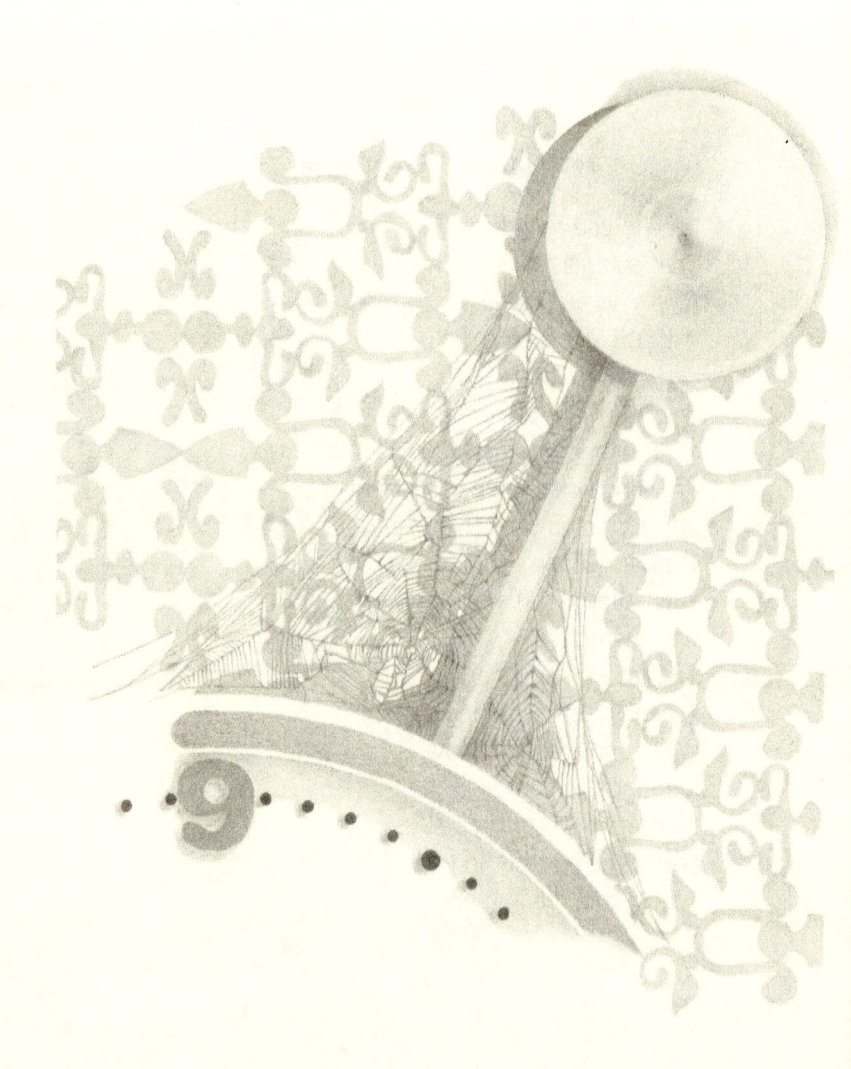

There is No Salt

There is no salt
    Like the salt on your skin
Give me your hand
    So I can taste the earth.
I need only this
Salt on my tongue
Earth in my hands
I am alive.

The Nature of Love

I can see inside you the flame of life
Burning tall and white
In an alcove of your body
Protected from the wind
It draws me to you
As I warm my soul in its heat
And touch the light in you
It comes back through me
A spreading wildfire
Uncontrollable blaze licking my core
It is the source of everlasting light
What we have all been seeking
I see your true essence
And in that, love revealed
I kneel before its power
May I be blessed
To carry this torch.

Chameleon

How is it that you are
All these chameleons in one human?
You are the boy of the jungle
Carefully moving branches aside to see sun falling on the
    forest floor
Returning to the city
The monk who travels lightly, owning only sandals
Then the sophisticate emerges, knowing just what to order
As the businessman in you takes a hurried call at the table
Becoming the strong father with glasses on, turning to his
    children
Evening falls as the man of the night appears, knowing which
    alley to enter
And then you are the nurturer, bringing me breakfast
As the lover in you wakens and we leave the food on the
    bedside table.
How can I know you?
Only as life splintered into a thousand pieces
Each one life itself
Let's not explain the mystery
Never tell me who you are
I don't ever need to know.

I Am Your Connection

You tell me
I am your connection to the world of women
Le monde des femmes
I ask you
Can I open it for you?
Have you enter straight within
Fully grown, full born.
Ripping aside the membrane
To step right in.
Can someone pass through this great divide
Go back in time
Before you were assigned your wrapping.
You are going to try this magician's trick?
Brave one
I will be your guide to this dark land
Hold my hand
As you are blindfolded already
It will be the journey of a lifetime.

The Genie in a Bottle

Like a genie in a bottle
Inside you
    is every man in the world
    in the green glass
    distilled into one person.
You carry it with you
wherever you are
    A second skin
    only I can see through
Like an Aladdin's cave
    Larger on the inside.
They are with you always
An elemental force
Contained under pressure
Through you I touch this
    contrast and power
Enchantment to hold in my hands.

The Body is a Temple

I have heard it said
That the body is a temple.
If that is so
Give me
100 lifetimes
to worship
your feet
before I move on
    to the rest of you
That endless field
flecked with wildflowers
Where do I even begin.

We Are Walking in a Cathedral

We are walking in a cathedral
Wherever we are
It is there
Above us and around us
This sacred place
That we bring with us
Wherever we are
The world without
Echoing the world within
Spilling onto the streets and trees
Flowers at our feet
A dream, not this
The veil lifted
To feel the powers within
Taking shape in the world before us
I open to this holy place.

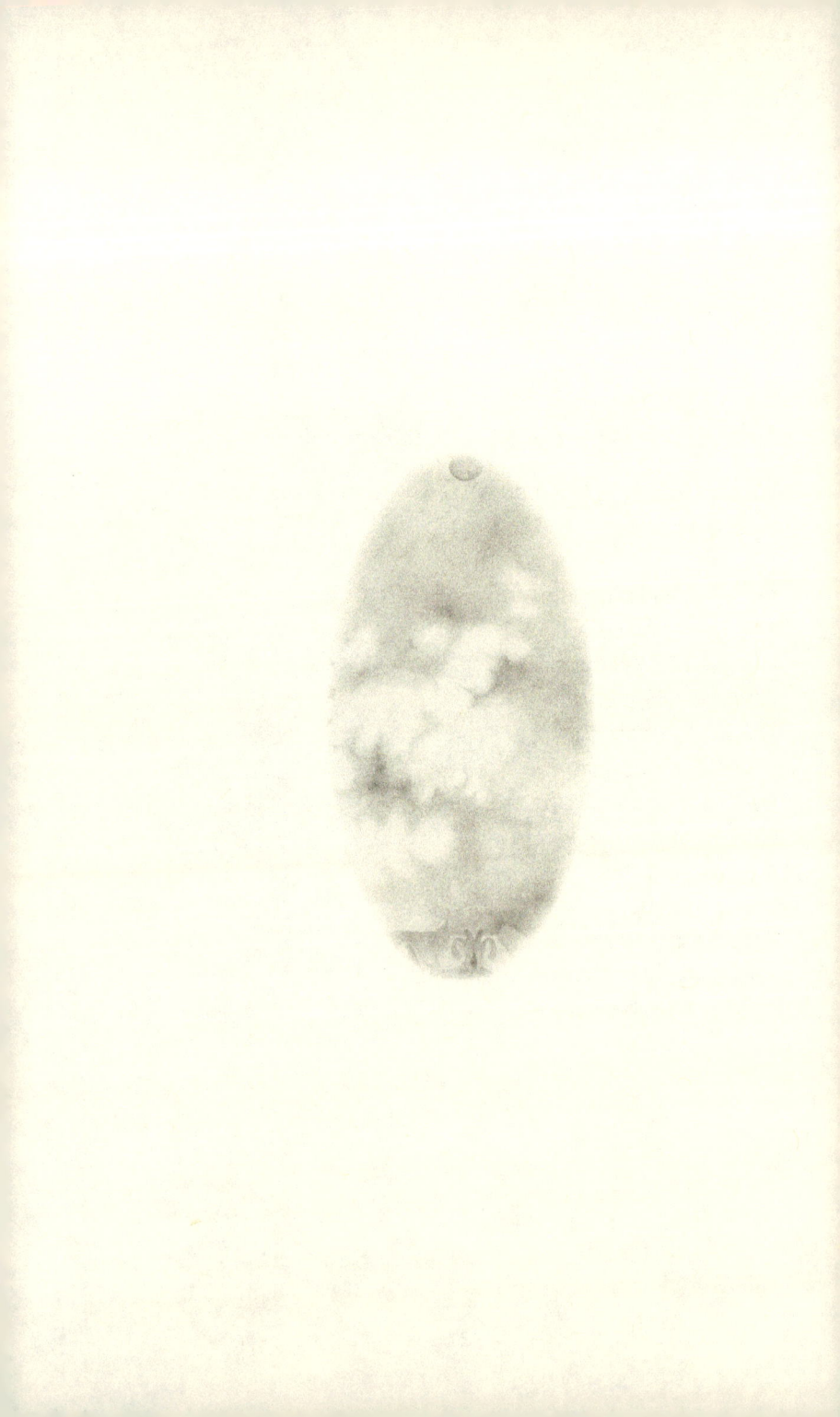

The Crystal

I am consumed
With fire
For the crystal
That is
Your collarbone
    Its smooth
      angular
      hardness
A universe in itself.
I must meet the carver
of such
perfection
Introduce me
Now.

The Principle

I want to be adored
Like Mother Earth is adored
Caressed like her flowers
Admired like her sunsets
Loved like her forests
Held like her oceans
    That is all I seek.
And then
To you I will return
Love like an elemental force
Sweeping all in its path
A tsunami of devotion
Like Mother Earth has for us.
    It is the order of the universe
    And the way of the heart.
Do you feel its power?

Immortal

I have decided
To make you immortal
It is my only power
But a good one.
I will do it in black ink
On white pages
You will live on
Like Shakespeare's Dark Lady
Only now it is time
For the dark Frenchman.
I am remembering
When we found each other again
And like lightning I was hit by the thought
That now that I had found you
That meant I would one day have to lose you.
The pain of that was carried within
Like a chariot pulled by two horses.
One, the joy of having
The other, the pain of losing.
Of course I choose
To ride the chariot
To not do so is even greater torment
That is the mud beneath the horses' feet
Where I would be trampled with the already half-dead.
And so I ride the chariot
As then I stand a chance
To touch divinity with my outstretched sceptre.
And finding you has also reminded me
Of the day my daughter was born
I held her
And a ray of joy struck me unlike any other

And in the next instant
Despair that I had her so late in life
I saw ten less years in her presence
and my own death, leaving her.
I had the same despair in finding you
But now the pain has subsided
Because I know the only truth
is that everything must change
And so in the having
There is always the unhaving
In the getting, the ungetting
And for now
We are together
And in that I will drown
as I make us both
Immortal.

The Silent Verse

I cannot tell you that I love you
Even if it be truth.
    I cannot write those words
    Or tell you with my tongue
They will not be said carelessly,
    As one might read them in a magazine
    Or hear them spoken on tv
    Or glimpsed in greeting cards
No, for once they are said
They will break me
    For all I have held together
    Will come rushing forth.
No porcelain skin can contain
The outpouring of my self
And the fear
    that there will be nothing left of me
    When those words are said.
And so
I am waiting
Only waiting
    For perhaps
    in the stillness of the darkest night
    When solstice comes creeping once a year
    In the transition between dark and light
    I will chance to tell you so.
And I ask you, should I then dissolve
Please
remember
I am
Boundless
love.

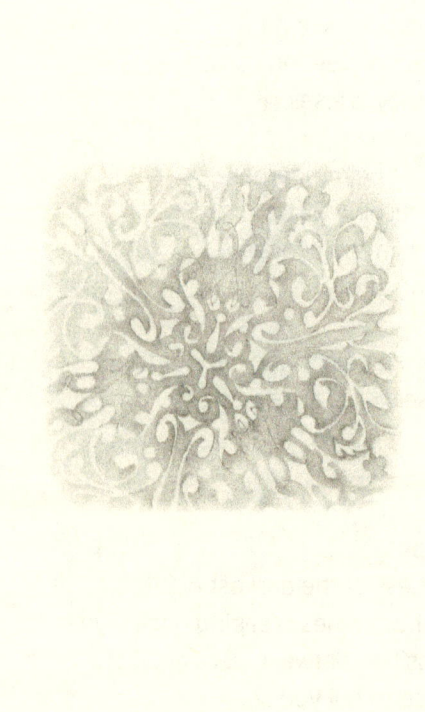

900 years

I remember
    When you said
It's like we have spent
    900 years trying to be together.
And my reply
    Was it only 900?

A Rose and its Thorns

We are now at the stage
where I can give you a rose
    and you understand
    and I understand
That we have chosen to leave the thorns on.
We are holding it in our hands
Admiring the red petals
    the intimate construction
    one petal curved around another
    protecting the centre.
At the same time, we are aware
that there is no protection
    the thorns
    are on the path
    of attachment
To be attached to you
    is to feel love and pain
So I give you this,
    With my eyes open
And I can promise
    that only in my humanness
    will I cause you pain
But never
from
my being.

Bring me Beauty

Bring me beauty like this
Every day, every moment
I am on my knees
There is a higher love
Breathing over us
Changing the world
Changing us.

There is a Portal

I know there is a portal
Somewhere around here
I saw it before in the silver light of dawn
When I aligned with you
And then together we aligned
With the entire universe
Stepping across the threshold
Where everything becomes the stream
Where there is no doing
Only being intensified
And we see ourselves with the squirrel, the bird and the cat
As nature has intended.
What key will reveal this opening?
It's like quicksand
Somewhere beneath me and around me
A field of energy swirling
As soon as my body and mind are willing to lie down
This is delicate work.
We stand here in the dim light, vehicles for each other.
I can sense that I must put my entire trust in you
Somehow I am the mouse
Who lets the elephant ride on her back
And in doing that
There is no question of who is stronger
Because it is the mouse's trust
That makes it so.
I'm only following the thread I was given
So don't talk to me of right and wrong,
of men and women
I only know the direction
And the flash in the night of this portal.

Where We are Going

Where we are going
No one can follow
We don't even know
Where we are going
I can't leave any description
(Because I'm just not that way)
And then there's your spelling
Which might be misread
We got rid of the map
It was all wrong anyway
And this place isn't marked
So I can't leave a clue
And it's all I can do
To close off all sounds
That might lead us astray
And whisper to you
It's this way.

The Sky and the Earth

We will meet at the horizon
   where the male in you
      becomes the sky above
   and the female in me
      becomes the earth below.
I honour you
   in divine union
together joined
   as the sky embraces the earth.

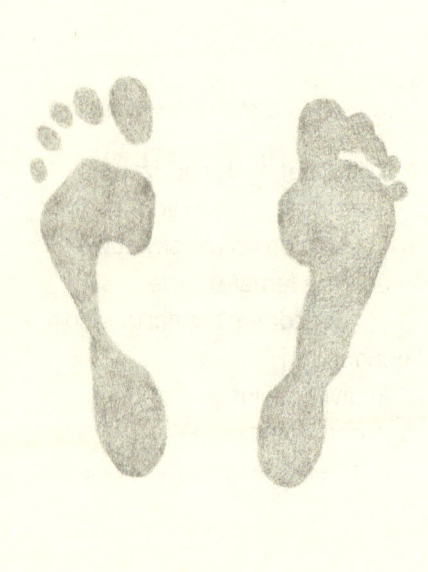

The Summoning

We must have summoned each other
    from deep within
A calling
    Not fully conscious
    Yet lying there
    Quietly breathing
Rising to the surface
    To call out from within the cosmos
A pure stream of asking
    Wanting only this
A connection like no other
No obstructions, no resistance
    A stream of light flowing outwards
And in the asking
No words
But like a child turning towards its mother
Clear direction
    Silent asking
        Deep understanding
And then you came.

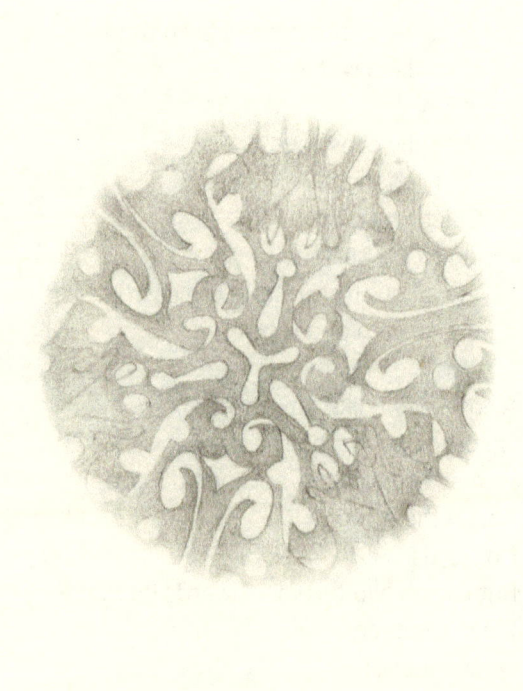

Hands

I feel his hands upon me.
No greater gift than this
Hands for living, working, making,
    Holding and caressing
Fingers wide, palms thick
    Salt upon his skin
Human touching human
Together walking in this life.

Sandcastles

I don't know how
We discovered this
It wasn't through any effort
Of our own
I never tried
And neither did you
So I can't lay claim
To any reward
Or tell others how to get here
It simply happened
Like we stepped into a hole on the beach
Dug by a child
And then once inside
We realized
It's a little different in here
And there's only one way to go
And then we began to dig
Throwing sand piles over our shoulders
Trusting it would all take shape.
We are now so well settled in our sandy domain
There is no looking back
But only more exploration of the path ahead
How far can we take this?

The Totem

You only have to look at me
    To understand my totem
The Cat in me
    Can only do this.
And I see that the Monkey in you
Must also exist.
Somewhere they are meeting
An intertwining
Animal worlds colliding.
    We are them and they are us.
    But I admit
    That the bits of kitty litter
    in my bed
    May be pushing things.
And can I ask you,
To please do something with those banana skins.
    And why are we moving so fast?

Somehow You Discovered this Trick

Somehow you discovered this trick
Of passing through me
My physical self dissolving
So that light falls on your head
With no shadow from me to block it.
There is no end to what you will find inside me
No barrier or stopping point
It merely flows from me and through me
But I am not the source.
There may be much more you will discover
A whole universe perhaps
And even beyond to the next
If there is one
You will find it
All we have to do
Is not think very much at all
And keep living in this endless present
Who knew it even existed
Like a hole drilled straight up and straight down
Infinitely expanding but never in width.

Did I ever tell you

Did I ever tell you
now I know what it is like
      to hold the hands of angels?
You surprised me with that
      when you kissed me.

Everything That Comes to Me

Everything that comes to me
Passes through you
And what comes to you
Passes through me
You are the way, the truth and the light
Could it be possible that we play this role for each other?
It's not like I see you
Living so far away
An illusionary force in my life
But then, I've never seen Jesus either.

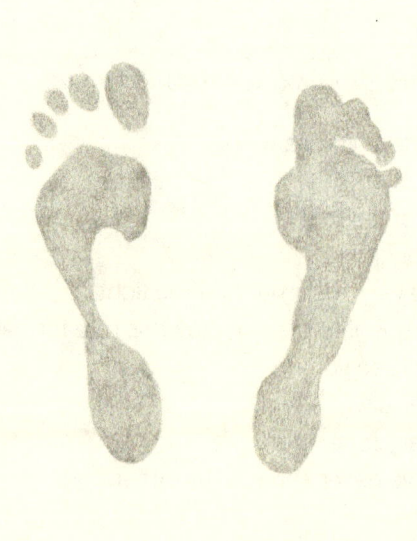

The Earth on My Skin

When you make love to me
You are making love to the earth
We are bound together
The same current, the same thoughts
I soften as the ground yields way
Damp mist rising upwards
The sun's rays pour through me
Bringing dormant ones to life
I reach out to hold hands with the leaves
My blood in tributaries that flow through my veins
I am anointed by the soil smeared on my skin.
When you love me
You love the earth
And when I merge with the earth
I return to you what I have learnt from her
I will tell you her dreams
When I know that you are listening.

The Other Way Around

You are the male
    And I am the female
And in the next lifetime
    I pray
That somehow
When it is the other way
    around
We will also
    remember
        it
        was once
        this way.

Guru and Teacher

The moment you merge
Into guru
Is the moment
I realize that nothing is
What it seems.

Still Being Consumed

Your collarbone
    is still consuming me
Because of its absolute
    singularity
How it sticks up
    beyond where others do
The bone almost bursting out of the skin
As though you were lifted up to the cosmos
by two clothespins clamped on your shoulders.
Maybe that is the same for all of us
The mark where the divine entered
is the part that conforms the least.

The Clouds Here

Look
Even the clouds are different here
    They hang in the air
        Like sheets on the line
        Billowing & round.
There are so many alternate worlds.
I want to explore them all
    With you by my side.
If only
we could leave
this hotel room.

I Have No Advice

You have no need of advice from me
and I have none to give
Everything you need
lies already at your feet
The path to unfold
    Uncurling your fingers
    You can see it there.
I am here in my perfect experience
beside you and with you
and part of you.
But never to tell you
and in that, we are free
in our perfect experience.

In the Garden

To live with you
is to recreate
the first woman
the first man
Holding hands in the garden
There is only you.

The Clouds

The clouds
   look like the
   turkey I just deboned
   All skeletal structure
      spine and ribcage floating by
      breastbone following
everything merging together
   earth reflected in the sky
      and sky reflected on the earth
      you into me, me into you
   under these clouds, yet part of them too
   in love with the sky, in love with you.

Two Halves and a Whole

A perfect whole
    which had to wait
    for its halves to be wholly complete
Before becoming one.
And so these two
    Lived their lives
    As separate halves
Until they reached a certain singularity
    Standing alone.
And only then could
    their world fuse
For the two halves to become one.
And being this
    to become more than one
As a walnut when cracked
    is two halves and a shell
And here they are now
    Soon to see, what is more than one.

Where is Your Vulnerability

Where is your vulnerability?
Where is it?
Mine is here, vested in my power.
Where is yours?
As you speak to me
I feel how yours crushes you
How it tears at you
Deflating air slowly
I want to take it in my hands
This tiny child of yours
You see how mine makes me bigger
More than myself
Yet part of myself
Yours is like a tiny munchkin
It can't be taken out too often
Your strength must be mainly what remains
You were made like this
And maybe as you get older
Your tiny child gets bigger
And mine gets smaller
Until finally
They are holding hands, the same size.

The Flames and the Fire

I wait for your experience
Sitting alone here by the fire
As I watch the flames
Have I looked at them before?
How they eat away the wood
Like an eagle picking a carcass
Until it is bare
A force of destruction
Bent on returning a body to the earth
Yet there seems a certain kindness
In those flickering wings
That flash so easily from yellow to orange.
And just as the meat becomes the eagle
The wood becomes the flames
I too become you
As night consumes the day.

You're Going to Cleanse the Last Part of Me

You're going to cleanse the last part of me
Aren't you
Rip out any tendencies that still remain
A thin shell of ego
    A certain resistance
    Hardening around a thought
    Hanging on with fingertips to old ideas
You'll do it with love of course
And a sharp exacto knife
You are the surgeon for the next part of my life
And to this, I will submit.

We Shouldn't Talk Too Much

We shouldn't talk too much
At least not in that vein
You know we can't explain
And let's not even try
We'll just sit here instead
At the window by the door
Let's let all the light in
I don't even mind the wind
I just know I can't go there
My mind doesn't work in spirals
I don't know what you're trying to say
So let's sit here by the window
And throw the rest away.

Nothing can keep us apart

Nothing can keep us
    apart
        not even
   our
   neuroses.

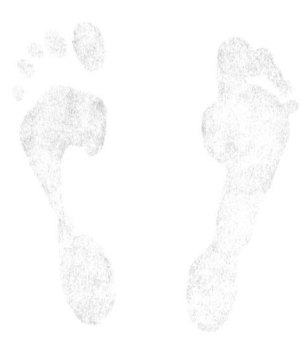

Returning to Our Homes

The separation
   comes
   as a tearing
      a ripping of fibres
      of wool felted together then torn apart
      a certain force to do this.
Where one begins and the other starts is not clear
Is this a type of Siamese twin surgery?
   Once fused together
   And now the tissues and vessels of the body are in pain.
Feeling this before my thinking mind
   can evaluate
      only temporary it might say.
Yet my body knows the truth
   that a laceration has occurred.
I can only follow this
   as I lie in the river
   and mend myself.

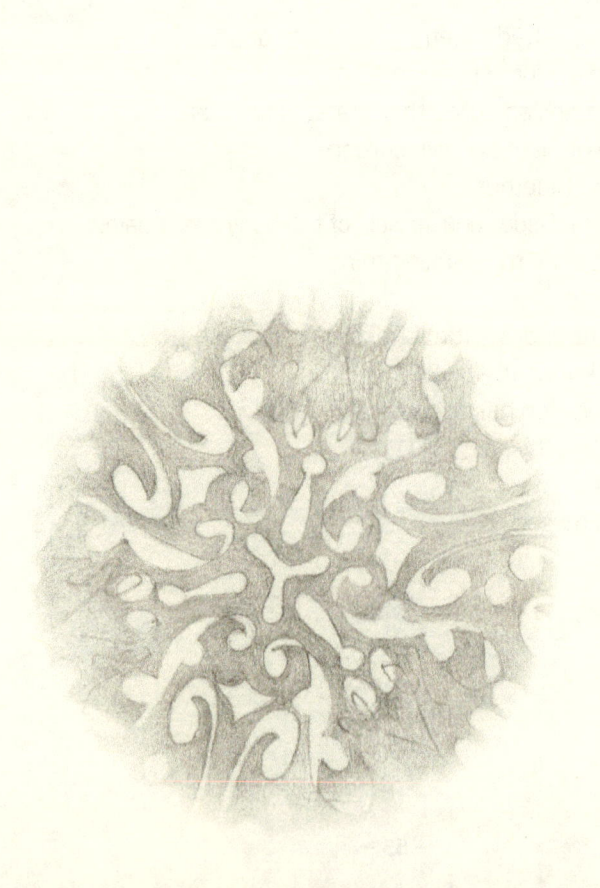

The Tap Drips

In the silence
the tap drips
    we were together
    and now we are not.
In the space between the next splash
before the water hits the sink
    I can accept
        This is how it is.
        It is this.
I can only say thank you
And know that in the deep acceptance
    lies my freedom
    And the taste of reunion
Before I dissolve into the impact
    and re-emerge again.

I Write You a Love Poem

I write you a love poem
While sitting on a stool in the kitchen
Seeing water boil in the cast iron
Becoming tumbling dolphins in the pan
The pulsing siren of the stove beeps
Music plays
My son calls out I'm done
The furnace breathes its long exhale
Through the vent beside me
All is living, breathing
Moving, stirring
Somewhere is your heartbeat.

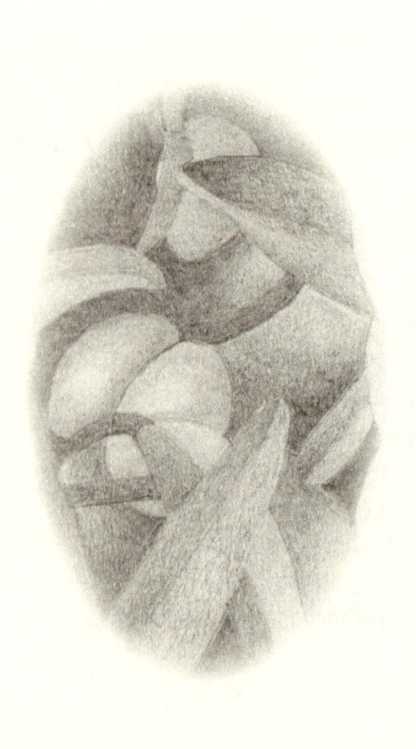

I See How in All Things

I see how in all things
Life flows through
And in that
an expression of each nuance of being
The fluidity of the water
Endlessly bending and pliant
The rocks beside the river
Tying me to earth
In never ending presence
And above them, green leaves in the breeze
Forever reaching out
May I be all these things to you
My body pliant like water
My presence shining into you
My words as constant as these rocks
And my hands fingered like green leaves
Always open for you.

The Flower and the Woman

Look at how the flower opens
Slowly, majestically
Like a woman opens to you
To be seen
Admired
Will you bless her with your words
Bestowed upon her radiance
That is how you treat her
As you would a flower.

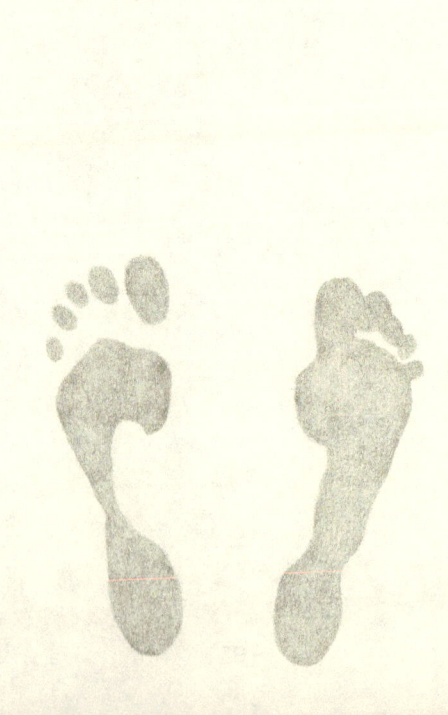

Watching

I am watching
    These men and women
    walk in the square
I am wondering
    When we will know our purpose
    Why we are men
    Why we are women
We are different for a reason
Can we feel what we are being asked to do?
It is arising
    Tendrils are coming from the earth
    Around our feet
    Tapping us on the back
We turn and there is no one there
Except our sense
    of why we are here.
Why did you return as a man?
Why did you return as a woman?
When I ask you this, can you know?
There are no words yet
So let's be very quiet
It is coming
on tiny silent feet.

Paradise Lost

I knew ecstasy
    once
I knew that elixir
    that ran through my blood
I was connected to all things
    through the one I love.
And now I sit
    and know that all things pass
I cannot be the fool that cries
Yet my heart is not hard
    Life washes over me
    Its salt upon my skin
I will emerge
    Still myself
    Maybe even slightly
    lighter
The thread of life pulls me forward
Yet I am no puppet on a string.
I will drink from life
    Its golden goblet in my hand
    Dark juice upon my chin.
I am as open
As a passageway with no door
Knowing there is more to come.

From the Author

Dear Reader,

Thank you for reading these poems. I'd love to hear your thoughts on this book, so feel free to leave a review on Goodreads or the website where you purchased it. Each review makes a big difference in my book being found and helps others who would enjoy these poems. I cherish every review that I receive. If you write one, a big thank you!

If you'd like to know when my next book is coming out, please sign up via my newsletter at annepepper.com.

Thank you,
Anne

About the Author

As a child Anne was called the cow's tail because she was always last. Despite being a dreamer, she managed to grow up to lead a practical life of earthly pursuits. Along the way she never lost her sense of the mystical element of life and it is from this that she writes. She has a degree in English Literature with distinction from McGill University and spent many years as a writer for other people. She also taught writing for several years in Vancouver at the University of British Columbia and at Simon Fraser University in the Writing & Publishing program. Anne lives in a small town in British Columbia, Canada and has three children.

www.ingramcontent.com/pod-product-compliance
Lightning Source LLC
Chambersburg PA
CBHW021116080526
44587CB00010B/543